A Conversation with
Archbishop
Rembert Weakland

Catholic Social Teaching and the U.S. Economy

A Conversation with
Archbishop
Rembert Weakland

Catholic Social Teaching and the U.S. Economy

Held on May 8, 1985
American Enterprise Institute for Public Policy Research
Washington, D.C.

ISBN 0-8447-3587-6

Library of Congress Catalog Card No. 85-072637

AEI Studies 430

Printed in the United States of America

The American Enterprise Institute for Public Policy Research, established in 1943, is a nonpartisan, nonprofit research and educational organization supported by foundations, corporations, and the public at large. Its purpose is to assist policy makers, scholars, business men and women, the press, and the public by providing objective analysis of national and international issues. Views expressed in the institute's publications are those of the authors and do not necessarily reflect the views of the staff, advisory panels, officers, or trustees of AEI.

Introduction

All the U.S. Catholic bishops under Archbishop Weakland's leadership deserve praise for the open process they have adopted in writing this pastoral letter: sending one draft out to be criticized, even to be battered about by the likes of us, and then another, before preparing a third draft. No other bishops in the world do that. Probably no other bishops in history have done that, and we want to thank all of them through you, Archbishop Weakland. You have set a marvelous example of an open church at work.

Under William Baroody, Sr., AEI began meetings between leading churchmen and leading businessmen some six years ago, and today we are continuing that tradition. We have conducted a bimonthly seminar on religion and economics here for some four years—many of these seminar's participants are here today.

Archbishop Weakland was very kind to the work of what those of us who serve on it call *a* lay commission. He agreed with us that our letter should appear before the bishop's letter. He was considerate and open throughout. For that, too, I would like to thank him.

I don't want to exaggerate too much how nice you were, Archbishop, because there were times when you gave as good as you got. [Laughter.] But we enjoyed that very much, too.

Archbishop Weakland has been the Archbishop of Milwaukee since 1977. For ten years before that he was the Abbot Primate of the entire Benedictine Order, some 31,000 monks around the world, and thus gained considerable international experience. Before that, when he was only thirty-six, he became archabbot of St. Vincent's Archabbey in "Arnold Palmer country," Latrobe, Pennsylvania, in 1963 near his family's roots. The archbishop was born in Patton, Pennsylvania, not far from the home of Monsignor Geno Barone, so well known and beloved here in Washington, and not far from my home in Johnstown.

After he studied music at Julliard, the archbishop adapted *The Play of Daniel* for the Pro Musica Antiqua for New York. It has been staged many times since 1958.

One thing not widely known about Archbishop Weakland, however, is that his family is legendary in all of western Pennsylvania, especially in our humble and beloved Cambria County.

The Weakland family dates back to the very first Catholic settlement in western Pennsylvania, Maguire Settlement, established in 1784. It was there, in Red Oak, where the gallant Russian prince, Dmitri Gallitzin, the first man to be ordained a Catholic priest in the United States, went to build a Catholic community in 1799, only to discover when he got there that the Weaklands were already there and part of the parish.

Oral tradition asserts that the Weaklands came over on the *Ark* and the *Dove* with Lord Cecil Calvert—for the first Catholic settlement in Baltimore in 1634. That tradition is very strong and is listed in a number of the parish histories of that area.

Archbishop Weakland is perhaps the first Catholic bishop among the descendants of that earliest vessel. Moreover, those of us who have watched him in debate will understand well that his great-great-great-grandfather, John Weakland, Jr., a tall man with black hair and high cheekbones, was known as the strongest man within a hundred miles of Loretto in any direction. He once wrestled a bear to death with his bare hands. [Laughter.] This is true.

On another occasion, John wrestled a wolf, gagged him, and brought him for his children to see. A stained glass window in St. Joseph's Church, the oldest church in western Pennsylvania, Hart's Sleeping Place, immortalizes the day when this same John Weakland, Jr., stood between a bunch of rowdy laymen who were threatening Father Gallitzin. With a fence rail held over his head he said:

> I have fought bears and other animals, it is true, but to date I have never, thank God, done harm to a human being. But now it looks as though something else might happen. Go home, because if there is any more monkey business or if anyone acts improperly about the House of God, or dares to lay hands on the anointed of the Lord, let him beware. As true as I live, I'll crush his skull for him.

With that, that first lay commission dispersed. [Laughter, applause.]

In the War of 1812 at the age of fifty-seven, John Weakland, Jr., volunteered for military service and marched all the way to Buffalo from Loretto, Pennsylvania, for duty and back again after the war. That suggests the endurance of the archbishop.

I can't forebear saying one more thing. Some years after John, Jr.'s death in 1854, his body was exhumed for reburial at the first Catholic church at St. Joseph's. When his coffin was opened, again according to the story, his right hand and arm, which had protected

Father Gallitzin, were alone uncorrupted.

You probably didn't know that this very embodied archbishop springs from so legendary a family. I am honored to present the first son of Cambria County, Pennsylvania, a great leader of the church, for his comments, after which we'll turn to all of you for the conversation which will ensue.

MICHAEL NOVAK
American Enterprise Institute

A Conversation with Archbishop Rembert Weakland

Catholic Social Teaching and the U.S. Economy

Thank you, Michael. I've had many introductions, but that one is truly unique. I would like to finish the story, though. After John Weakland saved the life of Prince Gallitzin, or at least made sure that he didn't get beaten up by those Irish, John was blessed by Gallitzin. The blessing, legend has it, was that some day one of Weakland's posterity would say Mass on this spot.

That little church is still out in the woods, abandoned now. Civilization went another direction. And so shortly after my ordination and my first Mass, all of the Weakland clan went out to that spot in the woods to fulfill the prophecy. My great-aunt Emma, who was ninety at the time, read the prayer of Anna, and said "Our Lord, you can dismiss me in peace, the prophecy has been fulfilled."

I would like to divide my remarks into just six brief categories. As a bishop I usually speak in categories of three—it's more traditional. Then I went to four in order to have a trinity and unity in the Augustinian fashion; now I've gone to six, and one of these days I'll arrive at ten, which Augustine said is the perfect number: three threes and one unity. Today, however, I want six categories.

Feedback on the Pastoral Letter

First, I am sure that nothing that has happened in the Catholic Church in the United States has produced as much feedback as this pastoral letter, much more than the letter on war and peace. The feedback has been not only voluminous, but also extremely thoughtful. Newspaper articles were the first feedback, and even those were helpful as an indication of what people are thinking across the nation. So often these responses begin with the complaint that the letter is far too long—55,000 to 60,000 words with the section on agriculture. Then, after noting its length, these same people have sent a hundred pages of comments with twenty-five points that were missed! At least the responses are substantial and should be very helpful.

The feedback from overseas interests me also. In South America and Europe, for example, the letter has inspired a lot of newspaper articles. In addition, the letter has been translated into German, Spanish, and Italian.

The response has not come just from the Catholic community: we have provoked as much interest in the Jewish community and other non-Catholic communities as we have in the Catholic. I find that very stimulating as well. Last evening I talked in a synagogue on Chicago's North Shore, for instance, and it was a good feeling to be invited there to talk about common problems.

As a bishop, though, in dealing with that feedback, I cannot simply count heads or do a computer study on the responses. What is important is to distinguish the voice of the Spirit in all that feedback. As a religious person, I have to approach it with this in mind. As we know, God can speak through just one whispering voice, and it is important that that voice not be neglected. This feedback demands reading, meditation, reflection in the light of the Gospel and of Catholic social tradition, and an attempt to hear the voice of God in that feedback. In that sense it differs somewhat from writing something for the *New York Times* op-ed page or the like. As bishops, we have to look at the material we receive in a little different light.

I have learned much through this whole process. My Lent consisted of taking the mail every morning and simply reading for an hour or an hour and a half through this feedback. [Laughter.] I did this early in the morning before the problems of the day got too heavy, so that I could reflect on it in a more prayerful manner. I hope we can keep that attitude toward the entire document, as we move toward the final product.

Biblical Teachings and Ethics

Second, I wish to address the biblical and the ethical section of the letter. When we began, we decided to keep the biblical section separate from the discussion of ethical norms and principles. Moralists are not happy with that approach, however. They feel that it is old-fashioned, because today's trend is to tie the biblical vision and the moral vision into one unity. We separated the two because we believe that the way in which we want to take part in the public debate, in the public square, is not primarily through the vision of faith as such. We prefer to sustain that vision of faith through a reasoned vision; therefore, we kept the so-called natural philosophy section separate.

In particular, the European critics have dismissed us as Americans, old-fashioned as usual, behind the times. They think we do not understand the political dynamics within which we are working. I would hope, though, that in a second draft we could at least show more connections between those two, rather than keeping them as totally separate entities.

If any section has received the highest praise, it is the biblical section. In the several meetings I have had with the Jewish community, they have rightly found that the Hebrew Scriptures are dominant in that section. In fact, many Jews have said to me, "What happened to St. Paul and St. Augustine?" We relied very much on the Hebrew Scriptures for the concepts in this section. This has given us a point of unity that we want to retain.

I believe we will have to do more work to tie that biblical vision into the ethical norms; perhaps that will have to be left for future scholars, however. We can only work within the state of present scholarship as we reflect on those two elements and how they bind together. I feel rather positive, despite some of the pressures. We will maintain the twofold division in the second and third drafts to keep our natural law theory, as it were, distinct from our faith commitment and hope that that arrangement will be helpful.

Shortcomings of Catholic Social Teaching

A third concern I have identified as weaknesses in Catholic social teaching—perhaps I should use the word *lacunae* rather than *weaknesses*. In our document the biblical section appears more coherent as a section than perhaps the one on ethical norms, simply because the one on ethical norms—particularly its analysis of economics—has never evolved into a holistic presentation.

In this sense, we have much to do in Catholic social teaching, and thus I do not see Catholic social teaching as a closed book. Our teaching has arisen mostly as negative reactions. The body of reflection that we have has developed within a historical context, and we have to see how it has evolved into what we have today. Of course, we expect this teaching to continue to evolve.

Some have rightly said that we were a little bit selective and did not present the whole of Catholic social teaching. Some have seen us as too rigid in dealing with that section. Yet we do want to see Catholic social teaching as something that can and will develop. For example, Leo XIII, in dealing with the problems of his day, 1891, was naturally concerned about two elements in society that worried him. The first was the plight of the industrial workers: the right to an honest family wage and the like. The second was the rise of statism and Communism and the need to balance those concepts with the tradition of private ownership. He responded to a historical situation as he reflected on problems of the day and brought Catholic social teaching to bear.

The same could be said of the *Quadragesimo Anno* of Pius XI in 1931 and the rise of Fascism. Here was a peculiarly Italian situation that forced reflection on the role of the state. That was where we got our first paragraph on subsidiarity. There is probably a little less of that particular concern in John XXIII, maybe a little less also in Paul VI. I think the *Laborem Exercens* of John Paul II comes out of the "Solidarity" experience and does have the same kind of historical roots.

In saying this, though, I am grateful to all those popes and others who have worked on Catholic social teaching over the past hundred years or so. Without that body of reflection, we would be in a very difficult position today. When I deal with the non-Catholic community in dialogue of this sort, they can sense that their denominations did not evolve that same kind of a social teaching. They have the "social Gospel" principles, but without the same body of reflection that we have in the Catholic tradition, coming from the end of the past century. Despite the fact that Catholic social teaching may have started as a response to particular situations, I see it as a great boon for us today in dealing with situations in which we find ourselves.

I also see this teaching as wonderfully Catholic. It clearly differentiates us from the fundamentalist tradition of religion, which is now entering into the mainstream. Although the Catholic tradition has always claimed its roots in a biblical vision, it has also always seen the need to bring into that tradition truth from wherever it might be found. Catholic tradition involves philosophy, science, and art, as a part of the whole. I see that biblical tradition reflected, then, through culture, through philosophy, and so on; that has been a part of our way of seeing things.

We are often slow in accepting truth from elsewhere, however. It took a long time, for instance, to vindicate Galileo within the Catholic Church. Although we are often slow, we do catch up. After going through a lot of turmoil over how a new truth can be integrated into tradition, we come out surprisingly well in the end. I am grateful for that tradition, and I think it is fairly clear in our document.

Government's Role and Subsidiarity

Together, Catholic social tradition and our document should illuminate two key subjects: the role of government and the question of subsidiarity. Maybe one of our next letters should address the role of government—how Catholic social teaching has a specific way of dealing with government and how that relates to the present moment, my fourth point.

Subsidiarity has also grown in the way that it is treated in Catholic social teaching. The first document that deals with it in any way is Pius XI's *Quadragesimo Anno,* paragraph 79. It begins:

> It is indeed true, as history clearly shows, that owing to the change in social conditions, much that was formerly done by small bodies can nowadays be accomplished only by large organizations. Nevertheless, it is a fundamental principle of social philosophy, fixed and unchangeable, that one should not withdraw from individuals and commit to the community what they can accomplish by their own enterprise and industry. So, too, it is an injustice and at the same time a grave evil and a disturbance of right order, to transfer to the larger and higher collectivity functions which can be performed and provided for by lesser and subordinate bodies.

When John XXIII dealt with that issue, he too eliminated the first sentence, which I think is interesting. I wonder what source book Father Pavan, the author who helped John XXIII, used for this. After Pope John quoted that paragraph 79, omitting the first line, however, he went on to say,

> It is obvious that recent advances in scientific knowledge and productive technology provide public authorities with far greater capacities than in the past for reducing inequalities among the various sections of production, among the various areas within the same nation and among the various peoples of the world. This development also puts it within their competence to control fluctuations in the economy and to bring effective remedies to bear on the problem of mass unemployment [*Mater et Magistra,* 54].

I cite this passage because these ideas will have to be clarified as we move into the next drafts of the letter. Arriving at a clear perspective on Catholic social teaching on subsidiarity and the relationship between government and private enterprise—between small and large, if you will—is very important. We should not neglect those texts where the role of the large is also accepted as necessary, especially as we move into a global economy.

Policy Sections of the Letter

To discuss my fifth point, I will briefly scan the second half of the document. The first half of the document that deals with the biblical vision and Catholic social teaching is then applied in the second half of the document to five areas. Originally, we had twenty-six areas that we wanted to deal with but found that, realistically, we could thoroughly treat only five. It really was a watershed because having worked through that first section, I said to the committee, Now as we go to apply these to concrete situations, which ones should we select? And of course, everybody has his hobbyhorse, even bishops, that each would like to see dealt with. When they all were put down on paper, we had twenty-six. And a word about that more toward the end because as you see that section of the document has to be by nature incomplete, and we know that. That's part of the built-in process. In fact, I'm amazed how people see the document as a whole when we really didn't see it quite that holistic at first. We saw it more as a body of doctrine with just five tentative, specific applications, while somehow the whole thing has come together in a way that went even beyond our expectations at the time.

For example, one of the bishops put down banking. We don't really deal anywhere in a specific way with banking. Taxation—we have very little in the document on the question of taxation. The family and the repercussions of the economy on the family. You could name the twenty-six. I needn't tell you that militarization of the economy was one of those which was also a part of the list.

We chose five specific topics because they seemed ones on which we had a tradition of speaking out, and also we thought we could deal with them adequately within the time frame allotted us.

The first one is employment. We are concerned about employment because it is the way in which the principle of participation in society becomes tangible. Our position was that if the identity of an individual is realized by active participation in society, then that participation through employment is very important.

We continually stress our fear that people will become complacent, satisfied with the unemployment rates that we have. We need to strive for a better participation rate. We believe that as we move into the next decades, this point will become salient. As we consider some of the predictions of such developments in technology as robots and automation and what these could do to the employment of the future, we must face these questions now, or the problems will become graver and graver. We are serious about that question of facing up to the unemployment problem.

Some have rightly criticized us for not analyzing the costs of what we are talking about, for not giving the trade-offs, and for not presenting our scheme in a way that would be economically satisfying to economists. They have a right to complain. If anyone is neglected in our letter, it is the economists, probably because our primary concern in writing these sections was to write as if the words came out of the mouths of bishops who are pastors, who teach, and who do not have economic expertise. We tried to avoid—and I think successfully—the need for a technical glossary at the end. In viewing that section, however, I think that we probably short-changed the professional economists who have questions that we did not answer. We may need an economic summary in conclusion to the letter as well as a pastoral one.

These comments also apply to the treatment of poverty. This section, I know, has often been called a new "Great Society" enterprise. We are aware of that criticism. We hope that many of the experiments made in the Great Society will be rethought and, where deficiencies do exist, they will be corrected. Especially in terms of subsidiarity, the government is certainly not the best provider of social services. The farther away from the hurt, the harder it is to see the solution. We certainly do not want to homogenize the poor. Here we were in one of our greatest binds in the document—specificity. We pleased nobody because we tried to adhere to a middle position. We found that this attempt brought us to a point midway between the speculative level and the policy prescription level: those who wanted no specificity were upset, and those who wanted it were upset.

We do want to avoid doing legislative work. Although we do not want to lay out details of specific policy, we do want to keep ourselves disciplined in relating our values and principles to concrete situations. That is how we see our text and the purpose of the exercise.

Our views on agriculture have been difficult to formulate. We must say a word about the immediate crisis, of course; at the same time, however, we have to try to go beyond that. One of the more complex aspects of the letter has been the necessity for addressing a given moment in the economy and at the same time for articulating durable values.

For that reason, the section on collaboration or, if I can use the dirty word, planning, has not attracted much attention. We see this chapter, though, as our opportunity to present ideas that could help shape a cooperative effort to reduce the human costs incurred as a dynamic economy moves ahead. Given its nature, this section is rather tentative. It does, however, describe some positive collaborative models that are working and that could work and does suggest a different way of economic decision making for the future.

In preparing the chapter on the third world, our committee was not agreed on how much of our document should address third world issues. Two bishops very much favored third world questions,

Bishop Rosazza and Bishop Weigand, who have had experience there. We finally agreed that some 30 percent of the letter should be devoted to issues of special interest to developing countries. Although this section has not yet been picked up much by our respondents except from the third world, we feel it is an important one and one that will require continual work as that situation changes. We included this section to show our global interdependence and to emphasize the importance of third world issues.

Ideological Values

My last remarks, my sixth, deal with something very personal; I speak here of what has happened to my vision through all of this. I have many friends in the third world, Africa, and in South and Central America, from the ten years I traveled those areas over and over again visiting Benedictines. The feedback from those friends and from those areas has been very interesting and also in a sense very encouraging. They see their own countries still tottering between what we might call American capitalism and a kind of neo-Marxism. They see themselves torn between these two ideologies. One friend from Brazil recently wrote saying that if capitalism could come to Brazil with the kind of values that our pastoral letter talked about, Communism there would be finished. That is a strong statement, but one implying that the image of capitalism is at variance with the view contained in the letter. The value system propounded in the letter is not evident in American-style capitalism, and yet it is just that value system that the developing countries are looking for. The letter, then, is an encouragement to us to continue this search for values because in this ideological struggle, I am positive that the one with the convincing values is the one that will survive.

I am reminded of Richard Nixon's remarks in a speech he gave in New York about two years ago. He said that when the Russians come into Central and South America they talk about values, they talk about brotherhood, they talk about work, and they talk about the dignity of the person. When we go into those countries, we talk about the evils of Communism. Hence, we need a positive approach there to be in any way victorious in that world struggle.

Questions and Answers

MELVILLE ULMER, University of Maryland: I am interested in your remark about returning to the practices of the Great Society.

Since 1970, when the Great Society expenditures reached their peak, outlays for means–tested programs for the poor have increased by 229 percent after correction for inflation. In real terms then, such expenditures have tripled. These outlays have done considerable good in relieving poverty and have also reduced the degree of inequality in the distribution of income. One analyst has estimated that the distribution of income went halfway toward perfect equality between 1960 and 1975. That's a tremendous change.

Along with the good have come some obvious ills such as the breakup of families as a result of welfare, the teenage pregnancies, and even crime. I wonder what you find in Catholic teaching that would enable us to make specific decisions about these things, such as you seem to think we should be making. People who have spent professional lifetimes with these problems have learned that we must speak with humility. Should we go farther? Should we change the pattern or not? There is tremendous disagreement on these matters. How is it that you can come to conclusive estimates of what ought to be done?

ARCHBISHOP WEAKLAND: I don't think we have come to conclusive estimates, but I think we do have a perspective. I would like to vindicate the Catholic Church's dealing with these problems.

We have a long tradition of dealing with poverty. I also think it would be helpful to listen to those who deal with it at the grass roots, because part of the problem is getting the information needed to deal with poverty.

Let me be specific. As I look at the people who come to our soup kitchens in Milwaukee—and they come in great numbers right now given the recent economic dislocations—I realize that all of those poor cannot be treated the same way. Each person is quite distinct, and each group is quite distinct. If you were to ask me how I would approach poverty in the light of our document, I would certainly put the person first.

I am absolutely convinced that we should not stint children in any way, because if we cut back on nutrition, for example, we are just creating problems for the future. To me, anything spent on helping those children to face life and to get an education is worthwhile. I believe that the way out of poverty is really education for almost all of us. That's how I got out of poverty, and, I think, that's how most in my generation came out of it. Education, to me, however, must be supported and developed.

The situation of the elderly poor raises totally different issues. That elderly poor group has to be dealt with specifically, especially elderly poor in rural areas that we know little about and have little contact with. The problems are easier in cities because the people are probably more pulled together than in the rural areas.

The group that worries me most—the group that very few people talk about or do anything about, and these I think are the real poor of our day—is the mentally disturbed. In most soup kitchens, for example, half of those people are mentally disturbed and couldn't hold a job if they tried. Giving them money without helping them beyond that leaves them vulnerable to exploitation by every person under the sun. The exploitation of the mentally ill in our society cries out for redress. I see this week after week in our soup kitchens. I can see the "preyers" hanging around those soup kitchens. I know of very few people who are doing anything more than putting food in the bellies of those people. One or two churches are trying to get psychologists and psychiatrists to give a little of their time to come on certain days to see if we can't begin to deal with that element in our society. I don't know what the laws are elsewhere, but in the state of Wisconsin these people are just thrown out onto the streets. I see this as a grave problem.

The structurally unemployed—Milwaukee's full of these right now—I'm sure can be taught new trades. Again, Milwaukee's full of people at age fifty-five who worked for Allis Chalmers for $30,000 a year and are now cleaning First Wisconsin Bank at night for $12,000. These are people that want to work, and I feel we have to do something to help them. Regarding the retraining of displaced workers, I said recently that it demands much of one psychologically and emotionally. For myself, for example, to go from monk to archbishop once in a lifetime is enough of a change, without having to be retooled again. The problem of structural unemployment should be treated in its own specific way.

Another serious problem we don't address at length in our letter is the suicides among the unemployed.

Poverty among blacks raises another set of specialized problems. Particularly troubling are the numbers of young black males who can't find or don't find work. I am not a great lover of Charles Murray's solutions in *Losing Ground*. I am not a neo-Malthusian who wants to throw people out on the streets and let them fend for themselves. I think our black community has problems that go beyond economics, and the solution to so many of these problems, it seems to me, is not economic. The solution lies in psychology and culture. We must look there to find our answers.

As I see it, the black problem in our own central city is the lack of role models. There are almost no role models for moving ahead for our blacks. I believe Michael Harrington's analysis of the black teenager is more accurate than Charles Murray's. Harrington identifies a tremendous fear of failure among the black youths and claims that they escape from that fear into welfare.

Role modeling is a very serious concern. I wonder if we shouldn't do some serious thinking about successful blacks and their responsibility to help the young in a way that perhaps we haven't yet thought of.

The same thing applies to the female poor, especially blacks, who have so many children out of wedlock. Again, to me, this problem is more psychological than economic, and part of it derives from the difficulty of the black male to take on the responsibilities of family life. The two factors are intimately intertwined.

Returning to your question, I think the church can help here and has something to offer beyond economic solutions or just throwing money at the problems. The key to solutions is with human beings and our dealings with each other—solutions require more cultural, sociological, and psychological approaches than economic ones. The Catholic Church has knowledge and experience that might be helpful to bring to bear on those situations.

HENRY BRIEFS, Georgetown University: As an economist, I was struck by your comment that economics had been neglected in the pastoral letter. That was the conclusion I reached after returning to a subject of early interest, namely the Catholic social ethics tradition. I want to point to a particular *lacuna* I find in the pastoral, which runs through other parts of the tradition: economic performance is taken for granted and viewed as static. Economic malfunctions, therefore, are looked at as lapses from what otherwise would be a perfect economy with full employment and zero or near–zero inflation.

The characteristic of our system in the past and the present—and I speak as an economic historian here—is precisely its dynamism. It does not consistently grow at a steady pace. Since 1947 this country has had employment and price stability as national goals, and we've had rather a tough go of trying to reach them. This has been the case in all kinds of conditions. It is true that in the 1950s and 1960s conditions allowed rather smooth economic growth. These were also the times in which social policies of the sort that the bishops advocate were readily attainable as the fruits of a well-functioning economy.

Unfortunately, we don't know how to make that animal behave that way consistently. It is not simply a matter of a lack of morals or political wealth. There are some intrinsic difficulties in the economic or technological dynamics.

ARCHBISHOP WEAKLAND: It's true that Catholic social teaching, including our letter, often sees the economic structure as static, rather than as a dynamic movement in which we enter at a certain point. You're absolutely correct in pointing that out.

The difficulty we face in examining values, such as we do in our letter, is that we do not want to write something applicable only to 1984 or 1985 or 1986. That's likely one of the problems—we want to create a larger vision of values and objectives, rather than making our decisions by our reactions to each individual situation. One gets the feeling so often in economics that it is too reactive to be conducive to positive thinking about the future. That's one of the things we are trying to avoid. We can't have it both ways. The need for values and objectives in a society and in an economic system is clear, even if at that given moment of history we cannot achieve them all. Perhaps this is a weakness in our own letter.

In our deductive reasoning processes, like good ecclesiastics, we begin with the vision and with the ethical principles because we think people need them and we think people have to live by them. When it comes to applying them in any concrete situation, however, we know that there are several options, which we point out in the letter.

Of course, there's more to it than that. The question is, At what point will we be satisfied and say that such and such is all we can realize of that vision at this moment of history? In other words, when should we be satisfied with a slice of bread when we cannot have the whole loaf at that moment? We probably don't go through enough of that kind of reasoning process in the letter, and we may seem to impute guilt to the business community and the economists for not realizing the whole vision when only a portion is possible.

Still, I would insist that the vision seems to be lacking. One of the messages we pick up now in the feedback from the letter is the enormous financial insecurity people seem to be living in, even if they are living well. That sense of insecurity comes especially from the middle class. Every time I pick up the newspaper, I find another economic indicator going up or down; people reading about those fluctuations week after week must live with a tremendous sense of insecurity about their own economic future.

Again, that uncertainty challenges the political and economic communities to maintain a certain degree of security among people, so that they can move ahead and exercise their freedom as they would like. Perhaps the letter does challenge you economists too much in that respect.

ERNEST LEFEVER, Ethics and Public Policy Center: The vision about which you have spoken so eloquently, I believe, is not unrelated to process. And that's my question. In the process of writing this letter, how do you handle the problem of diversity—the diversity among the bishops and the diversity among the immediate writing staff? Has the process so far yielded sufficient diversity to reflect the richness of American life and thought? How do you avoid accommodating diversity by going to the lowest common denominator?

As a Protestant, I am aware of the problems in this respect related to the National Council of Churches and the World Council of Churches, because they too have diversity and need to make pronouncements.

ARCHBISHOP WEAKLAND: In answering that, I would like to distinguish the process from the tradition and the content. I think maybe I could do that easily.

We use and want to continue to use the open process that Mr. Novak spoke of; that's so important to us. That process itself is an education, helping people formulate their own thinking as well. Especially for us Americans, we want that kind of educative process, because we learn by doing rather than by having something just handed to us pat and finished. The process is important in getting people to think about issues to which, up to now, perhaps, they had not given serious thought. I like to use music as an example here. I think it's important in musical training for everybody to join the chorus, for everybody to belong to the band, and for everybody to have that practical experience of involvement in music. Although no one will compose Beethoven's Fifth Symphony through that process, it does help people to form an appreciation for and an understanding of what music is all about.

When it comes to the ultimate document, we bishops will try to remain bishops; that is, in the structure of the Catholic Church, our teaching role and authority are such that we feel we must come to a consensus on what we can and publish it to help our people form their spiritual lives and consciences. That comes at the end, however. As we go through this process we want to be able to get as much pluralism as we can from the community, reflect on it, and yet at a certain point we have to vote, to come to a conclusion.

Now, I hope that in that third draft, the different levels of our speaking will become clearer.

People will have to become more sophisticated about these

matters. When we talk about biblical vision and our ethical principles, we say it with a lot more force than perhaps if we are discussing policy options. Catholics will have to get used to reading our documents in a more diversified way, and I think that's a help. This approach is not only a help to our document, but also a help to any kind of papal teaching.

In the Catholic Church we have always had all kinds of degrees of teaching. For example, if the pope speaks in an encyclical letter, the letter has a certain weight about it. In labeling the piece an encyclical letter, the pope is trying to put a maximum weight on its contents. Even at that, everything in the letter may not be equally true. It simply means, however, that it is what the pope, at a moment of history, thinks is very important for the Catholic Church. If he calls it an apostolic exhortation, it carries less teaching authority. If it's a weekday homily at St. Peter's, it carries a yet lower degree. And who knows what he says in his private chambers. [Laughter.]

We have to get used to those different levels of teaching authority within the church. I believe we are becoming more sophisticated in differentiating among these levels, being forced to do so perhaps by our writings. People will have to begin to sort these things out for themselves. I find that healthy—I find it very healthy for the church to do that. It's also the way in which growth can take place within a church. Growth does not occur if everybody thinks alike. That pluralism that you talked about is absolutely necessary. Even if an idea does not find its full realization in this version of the letter, we feel that if it's of the Spirit, it will eventually come forth and will influence all of us.

So often I've had that experience in my own life as a monk. When I returned to the monastery after studying in Europe in 1951, I'll never forget an old monk who got up, said something in chapter, and was hissed. He was the prophet of his day; he didn't get bitter or angry. His was a voice, however, that ultimately prevailed. Whether it's the minority or the majority, if the voice is of the Spirit, eventually it comes through.

MR. LEFEVER: Just one clarification, Archbishop. I was referring also to the diversity among the bishops themselves who participated in the writing process and their immediate staff. Do you think that they provided sufficient diversity in that process behind closed doors to represent the richness of American life and thought?

ARCHBISHOP WEAKLAND: Yes, we should have you listen to it sometime. [Laughter.]

I often feel that it would be easier if it weren't so diversified! It's less demanding to chair a committee where there is not quite so much diversity. We've all grown in the process, of course, and I'm sure we've all changed positions greatly through contact with each other.

It is true that among the drafting bishops we don't have the diversity that the bishops of the peace pastoral had. We're probably not quite as far apart in our thinking processes as they were, but we have enough diversity to maintain a constant and good dialogue. We believe that we have compensated for that lack of diversity by our hearings and with the feedback process.

ROBERT SIRICO: I am a Paulist seminarian studying at the Catholic University of America and I want to begin by reiterating what Mr. Novak said about the open process that the bishops have embraced in the Peace Pastoral and now this one. In my own formation, I've learned so much about church teaching from what the bishops are saying.

There are, however, some areas that I'd like to probe with you, Archbishop. In the document and in your remarks here you speak of the principle of subsidiarity. Could you go a little farther in saying what you expect to come out in the subsequent drafts?

In paragraph 184, for example, where you concern yourselves with job creation strategies, perhaps you missed an opportunity there to apply the principle of subsidiarity in inner city private enterprise zones or other ways in which the economy can be built without government intervention as we move away from a centralized approach to economic planning. In addition, regarding the problem of black unemployment, have you considered some of the ideas that Thomas Sowell has written about? He speaks of the deleterious effect of well-intended programs like minimum wage regulations on black teenagers.

Then, too, would you comment on the rumor that the document is divided into two parts to accentuate the diversity of opinion on the handling of wealth?

ARCHBISHOP WEAKLAND: In response to your question on subsidiarity, I hope that our document will make that issue a little clearer. We are not saying that small is beautiful. We are not Schumachers in the document. On the other hand, we are not saying that big is bad. We believe that government, even when things are delegated to a lower level, doesn't relinquish its accountability and concern for what happens there. I think the popes always admit, and we will have to say this clearly, that there are many things that can be done only at the governmental level. Our world is too big and too complex for us to delegate everything to the smallest unit.

Probably more can be done for unemployment and poverty by subsidiarity than for any other problems, if it can get close enough to the problems themselves. In terms of other solutions, I am very interested in the private enterprise zones you mentioned. These appear to have a lot of potential, and it's one of the things on which we're meeting in Milwaukee to talk about. I think the zones have a lot to offer. While I'm not sure that the document has to deal with them specifically, I think they are an interesting and good possibility. The problem is larger than private enterprise zones alone can cure, however. The whole transportation and communication questions in the black communities must be resolved.

As for the black teenagers, I do not know if we will address their problems specifically; maybe we should. Perhaps we should treat these problems like an area, rather than so broadly and see if we can come up with some more solid solutions that don't just waste money, as Thomas Sowell would point out. I'm not sure how specific we want to get as we move into programs of that sort.

As for the question of the theoretical and practical areas and the diversity existing in the latter, I feel strongly on this subject. The first draft was a wonderful exercise for all of us in trying to keep us consistent between principle and practice. I wonder, though, if it also may have been just too simplistic at times and if maybe we shouldn't reword it in a way that doesn't make the assignment sound too easy. Until the letter reached the public forum, we didn't realize that the division would be so neat in people's treatment of it. In the next draft we are trying to do away with that kind of simplistic approach, but there's no way of doing away totally with the deductive methodology, even if we recast it in a more inductive fashion.

PHILIP WOGAMAN, Wesley Theological Seminary: As a Protestant theologian, I should find more to object to in the document than in fact I do. I want to express a very great appreciation for it, in particular for the serious and profound implications of the criterion of community participation, which unaccountably many of the critics of the document have missed, I think. That criterion puts the focus beyond sole reliance on economics and material factors and helps to point up what you have stated elsewhere in the document—the instrumental character of all economics, serving what are ultimately spiritual values and in a sense community values as well. That theme is also very important in Protestant theology and social ethics.

I wanted to ask for your comments on the possibility of an ecumenical dialogue emerging from the document, which many Protestants as well as Jews and others have viewed with great appreciation.

ARCHBISHOP WEAKLAND: Since it's permissible to brag, this is probably the first time in preparing a document that we felt it absolutely necessary to get the ecumenical input before we started. Most of the time we prepare the document first and then hope that the other groups will accept it. This time, however, the ecumenical community was totally involved in the process itself. In our hearings, I don't think we even questioned a person's faith if we thought we needed his expertise.

Our feedback has also been very ecumenical. Perhaps the next stages should have built into them a kind of ecumenical implementation so that we can begin to think about how such a dialogue would and could happen. I see interesting possibilities in the future in that area, with Protestants as well as with the Jewish community. I've been overwhelmed by the support the Jewish community has given us. I wonder if perhaps the reason why this is happening in the Catholic Church is that Vatican II brought us a new biblical dimension. The readings now from the Hebrew Scriptures, which we had not used in public before, have brought a new biblical awareness into the Catholic Church from its Judaic roots. Even in the new songs that are written, I notice many Old Testament words, mostly from Isaiah and the prophets. Just recently, I preached a sermon in the cathedral where I alternated paragraphs from Amos the Prophet with paragraphs from John Paul II at Yankee Stadium, without telling the people where it came from. It was amazing to see the relationships between these two. I think the congregation was a little flabbergasted when they found whose words they had been hearing.

I couldn't have preached something like that in my young priesthood; it would have been impossible: nobody would have known Amos. We followed a different style of doing things then. Now I preach on the Hebrew Scriptures as much as I do on the New Testament. This new emphasis on the Old Testament has also altered our attitude toward this world more than we realize. Some people said that we Catholics were becoming more earthy—I hope in a good sense. Vatican II brought the realization that the Kingdom of God is worked out in this world and not delayed, so that what happens here to create a just world is a part of working toward the kingdom. That concept has become a reality for Catholics. What we don't want to do is to fall into the Social Gospel, becoming so involved in our work that we lose the biblical inspiration. Here, in the ecumenical dialogue, I'm convinced that the Catholic contribution is in the sacraments and in the symbolism that keeps that element so constantly visible that the inspiration comes from the worship element.

THELMA LEVINE, George Washington University: As I understand the letter, the bishops have been offering, in the words of a famous continental sociologist and historian, a diagnosis of our time. That diagnosis of our time is a diagnosis of America and its time. Not only have the bishops done that, but also they have offered a prognosis showing how the problems of our time should be dealt with.

Moreover, your effort to offer a diagnosis and a prognosis is presented in terms of values. How have you related your diagnosis and prognosis, in terms of values drawn from the great Catholic tradition, to the American religious tradition, going back to the Puritans, moving through the great American Enlightenment into the great days of American romanticism and transcendentalism and finally into pragmatism and naturalism? To what extent have you considered the relationship of these Catholic values to what can be seen as the distinctly American tradition of values?

ARCHBISHOP WEAKLAND: Excellent question. We have thought about this relationship probably more than the letter shows. We have said very little about it, and we were prodded a little bit by a certain lay document to think more about it. [Laughter.]

We can look at the question in several ways; let me do it in layers.

One layer would be this: how much has the philosophy of the Enlightenment influenced Catholic social teaching? The answer is probably more than we would be willing to admit. In the past century when Leo XIII began his reflections on the dignity of the human person, on private ownership, and the like, he relied a lot more on John Locke than on Thomas Aquinas. That element of Aquinas comes in only with John XXIII, when he puts the common good first and then after that private ownership, vindicating private ownership only if it supports the common good.

What would also be interesting is to study the whole language pertaining to human rights, which has become so important now in Catholic social teaching. How much of this concern for rights comes out of Enlightenment philosophy rather than the medieval or Renaissance Catholic tradition? I think we would have to be up front and say that we really took this from the Enlightenment era. That kind of question does not belong in a pastoral letter, although it surely belongs in the academic analysis of where we are and what we are doing.

I could mention several other ideas that were there at the beginning of U.S. tradition, were set aside, and are now coming back in via Catholic social teaching. Thomas Paine's writing on the rights of the human person are very interesting and seem to be exactly the list of rights that John Paul II gave at the UN. An author like Paine, who somehow got lost, is now coming back again through a strange channel. I think this is a very fruitful development, and my own interests are whetted by a document of this sort to examine that development. Even a phrase that some didn't like, "economic rights," for example, can be found in U.S. tradition.

Having said that, though, I give my caveat: I'm sure there are areas especially those that deal with communitarian values, where our letter and Catholic social teaching will be at variance with American civil religion. I think that's inevitable, and I say that up front. Although I tried to analyze the differences in a talk several months ago, I was not very successful because I was going by instinct. I often go by instinct, rather than working a problem out analytically. I believe that somewhere along the line that kind of argumentation will have to be laid out clearly. At what point are we calling into question certain values of American civil religion that are there? We feel at this moment in history that it is very important to balance the good individualistic tradition with a component of communitarian values. Some might not like the way we do it; they might call it Socialist because they believe it goes too far. Still, we do sense that need at this moment of history.

Last night in speaking in a Jewish synagogue in Chicago, I used an old Jewish midrash. I started by saying that there were three Jews in a boat. The rabbi corrected me, saying that the midrash says there are three *persons* in a boat. It's nice to know that it's not one Catholic, one Jew, though, and one Presbyterian. . . . [Laughter.]

These three are having trouble getting along in the boat because they're fighting over territory. Finally, they decide to divide the boat into three. Each one gets a section: each one can paint his section of the boat the way he wants, can hang his underwear the way he wants it to dry, and everybody's happy—until two of them see that the third is boring a hole in his section of the boat. At that point the other two say, "We're in this boat together."

Now, what we're saying is at certain points in history there's a need to assert that certain communitarian values have to be put into action; otherwise, the boat might take on water.

ALLAN PARRENT, Virginia Theological Seminary: How do you and how does the document understand the relationship between policy, recommendations and the lay apostolate—that is, those who will carry out their Christian vocation in areas where decisions on these issues and questions are made?

ARCHBISHOP WEAKLAND: I understand it this way. In terms of teaching, the bishops have a very specific role. I understand also that in that teaching process, they have to hear from everybody, and that's what we are in the process of doing, especially those who are in the field.

I also hold that in matters of policy, in trying to apply the Christian vision to actual life, the clerical element has much to contribute and should be a part of that mix and that dialogue and not suffer from it. In other words, to divide the territory and say that bishops deal with theory and lay people deal with practice to me is unreal.

The Vatican II distinction is this: bishops and lay deal with theory, although bishops have the final pronouncement. When it comes to acting out policy in the public arena, then the lay person is the one who is active, not the bishop. That's why priests are prohibited from running for office: public office is a lay component, not a clerical.

That division is easy in theory and sometimes rather difficult in practice. My feeling is that we as clerics have to be very clear about not being political figures. I find this is very difficult for me—I'll have to admit—because in the past months I have often been pitted against a politician by a TV interviewer. I always have to say to myself, "Rembert, you're preaching the Gospel; Rembert, you're preaching the Gospel. That's your job; don't get out of the role that is important."

I don't think it's wise to say, however, "Rembert, you don't know a thing about the active part of it." I have some reflections there that are valid, but I would be hesitant to want to change roles and become an implementer of policy.

I don't know if that's helpful, but I would say the Vatican II split is more in action in the world for lay rather than dangling in the realm of the theory and thinking.

William Marshner, Christendom College: Archibishop, I have a question about that moral vision that you say is central to your work. In paragraph 21 of the document and also in the summary, you state your fundamental norm: namely, in evaluating an economic decision or policy, the question is, What does it do for the poor? How does it affect the poor?

Now, as that norm reads, it is an overtly consequentialist norm. You're saying, it seems to me, that in evaluating a policy, we have to see what its total impact, good and bad, would be on the poor. Then, if the net effect is better than the net effect of an alternative policy, then we have to adopt the first policy. Many people would point out that there is an enormous empirical difficulty about predicting what the consequences will be for any policy.

I want to draw your attention, however, to what seems to me an even more fundamental difficulty: namely, that there is no objective way to weight the several effects. Without an objective series of weights to put on the positive and negative effects, I don't see how it is possible for me or for anyone else to apply the norm. The problem with the fundamental norm is how it can be applied in the situation at hand.

We have a decision to make in American economic policy: do we continue heavy funding through the public sector to relieve problems of the poor, or do we cut back on that heavy public spending to try to promote greater investment and greater job creation in the private sector? Both of those would affect the poor, but it seems to me that without an objective series of weights and measures, it is impossible under your norm to decide which of those two policies is better.

Although perhaps my difficulty is overdrawn, I would like to hear your reaction to it. In particular, do you agree that your norm is consequentialist in character?

ARCHBISHOP WEAKLAND: As for the point about consequentialism, in a sense we do examine effects. We chose this at the beginning because we decided not to take capitalism as a theory and just analyze theoretical capitalism. Once we made the decision to deal with the effects of capitalism on the society, yes, we were then consequentialist. That decision, I think, was very important in our thinking processes.

The French bishops have been highly critical of that approach, saying that we should have dealt with *l'essence de la capitalisme*. We decided against staying at such an abstract plane, instead dealing with the effects that an economy has on the life of people. Our primary interest is how that economy affects the quality of lives of the people and in particular of the poor.

In weighing one policy against another, I believe we must bring to bear the research and knowledge available at that moment. This is true for anybody making any decision, of course. We have to weigh one course of action against another and decide which one best embodies our principles. We do that all that time.

MR. NOVAK: Archbishop Weakland, we at AEI thank you very much for your generosity, your candor, and your openness—as do all our guests.

SELECTED AEI PUBLICATIONS

Speaking to the Third World: Essays on Democracy and Development, Peter L. Berger and Michael Novak (1985, 59 pp., $3.95)

The Global Debt Crisis: America's Growing Involvement, John H. Makin (1984, 281 pp., $18.95)

How Does the Constitution Secure Rights? Robert A. Goldwin and William A. Schambra, eds. (1985, 125 pp., cloth $13.95, paper $5.95)

The Church and the Social Question, Franz Mueller (1984, 158 pp., $14.95)

Are Wo … Zinsmeister, eds. …

Freedon …

Small C … *etries,* Mark Falc …

• *Mail* … ITUTE, 1150 Sevente … *nd handling, add 10* … *e on prepaid orders)* … *all toll free* 800-424 … *change without not* …

The A … competition of ideas … objectives: (1) to e … to increase research … he academic commu … The areas studied … olicy, Fiscal Policy, … rams, Legal Policy, … nd Religion, Philoso … receive

- a s … ivities
- the …
- a 3 …
- a 40 percent discount for certain seminars on key issues
- subscriptions to any two of the following publications: *Public Opinion,* a bimonthly magazine exploring trends and implications of public opinion on social and public policy questions; *Regulation,* a bimonthly journal examining all aspects of government regulation of society; and *AEI Economist,* a monthly newsletter analyzing current economic issues and evaluating future trends (or for all three publications, send an additional $12).

Call 202/862-7170 or write: AMERICAN ENTERPRISE INSTITUTE
1150 Seventeenth Street, N.W., Suite 301, Washington, D.C. 20036